The
FRENCH
Kitchen Cookbook

First published in 2012

LOVE FOOD is an imprint of Parragon Books Ltd

Parragon
Queen Street House
4 Queen Street
Bath BA1 1HE, UK

ISBN: 978-1-4454-7856-2

Printed in China

Design by Tracy Killick
New photography by Clive Streeter
New food styling by Teresa Goldfinch

Notes for the reader

This book uses both metric and imperial measurements. Follow the same units of measurement throughout; do not mix metric and imperial. All spoon measurements are level: teaspoons are assumed to be 5 ml, and tablespoons are assumed to be 15 ml. Unless otherwise stated, milk is assumed to be full fat, eggs and individual vegetables are medium, and pepper is freshly ground black pepper.

The times given are an approximate guide only. Preparation times differ according to the techniques used by different people and the cooking times may also vary from those given. Optional ingredients, variations or serving suggestions have not been included in the calculations.

Recipes using raw or very lightly cooked eggs should be avoided by infants, the elderly, pregnant women, convalescents and anyone suffering from an illness. Pregnant and breastfeeding women are advised to avoid eating peanuts and peanut products. Sufferers from nut allergies should be aware that some of the ready-made ingredients used in the recipes in this book may contain nuts. Always check the packaging before use.

Picture acknowledgements

The publisher would like to thank the following for permission to reproduce copyright material on the following pages:

Linen backgrounds, textured borders and decorative frames (throughout): Fotolia/Tombaky; CG Textures; Fotolia/Robynmac.

Contents

Introduction

The French – be they young or old, sophisticated urbanites or rural agricultural workers – have a special place in their hearts for the unpretentious, hearty and satisfying food which epitomises their national cuisine. French food showcases the best of fresh, seasonal ingredients and is inevitably accompanied by a good selection of wines.

To compliment a delicious French meal it's important to capture the relaxed ambience which we associate with all good bistros, brasseries and indeed home-meals in France. That iconic image of a cosy neighbourhood restaurant, with a zinc-topped bar, paper or chequered tablecloths, flickering candlelight and the daily specials displayed on chalkboards may not be quite right for everyday eating, but you can certainly capture the charming buzz of playful chatter that accompanies great cooking in France.

Traditional, home-style dishes, such as Coq au Vin, Cassoulet, Boeuf Bourguinon, Soupe à l'Oignon and Croque-monsieur, with their solid roots on bistro menus up and down the country will become a much-loved part of your repertoire.

It is the simplicity of French food that makes it ideal for re-creating at home. As you look through this beautifully photographed collection of tempting recipes you will find familiar ingredients and basic cooking techniques. This is not the food of Michelin-starred kitchens, it is food to enjoy with family and friends.

Bon appétit!

chapter one
Starters

Soupe de poissons
Fish Soup

❖ Serves 6–8
❖ Prepared in 20–30 minutes, plus chilling and standing
❖ Cooks in 1½ hours

100 ml/3½ fl oz olive oil
3 onions, roughly chopped
3 carrots, roughly chopped
3 celery sticks, roughly chopped
1 fennel bulb, finely chopped
6 garlic cloves, roughly chopped
1 bay leaf
150 ml/5 fl oz Vermouth
2 thyme sprigs
1 kg/2 lb 4 oz whole fish, such as sea bass or
    pollack, gutted, filleted, but bones reserved

1 kg/2 lb 4 oz bones from white fish
250 g/9 oz unpeeled prawns
2.5 litres/4½ pints water
juice and zest of 1 orange
pinch of saffron
toasted slices of baguette and grated
    Parmesan cheese, to serve
salt and pepper

Rouille
25 g/1 oz fresh breadcrumbs soaked in
    1 tsbp water
3 garlic cloves, roughly chopped
1 egg yolk
1 red chilli, deseeded and chopped
½ tsp salt
200 ml/7 fl oz olive oil

one Place a large saucepan over a medium heat and add the olive oil. Add the onions, carrots, celery, fennel, garlic and bay leaf and cook gently for 20 minutes, or until soft. Add the Vermouth and thyme and simmer for 2 minutes. Add the fish, fish bones and prawns and increase the heat. Cook, stirring, for 5 minutes, then add the water, orange juice and zest and saffron. Bring to the boil and simmer for 45 minutes. Remove the bay leaf.

Two Meanwhile, make the rouille. Put all of the ingredients, except the olive oil, into a food processor and process to a paste. Keep blending and add the olive oil in a slow stream until the consistency is that of a thick mayonnaise. Put in the refrigerator to chill.

Three Crush the bones by processing the soup in batches in a food processor or blender. Leave to stand for 20 minutes. Strain through a colander first, then through a fine sieve, then pour into a saucepan. Season to taste and reheat again to serve.

four Serve immediately with slices of toasted baguette topped with grated Parmesan cheese and bowls of rouille alongside.

Potage St Germain

Pea Soup

✤ Serves 4
✤ Prepared in
   15–20 minutes
✤ Cooks in 20–30 minutes

40 g/1½ oz butter
4 tbsp finely chopped shallots
1 litre/1¾ pints vegetable
   stock or water
400 g/14 oz shelled peas
pinch of sugar
4 tbsp crème fraîche
salt and pepper
croûtons and blue cheese,
   such as Roquefort, crumbled,
   to serve

one

Two

Two

one Melt the butter in a large saucepan over a medium heat. Add the shallots and fry, stirring, for 2–3 minutes, or until soft. Add the stock, peas, sugar, and salt and pepper to taste and bring to the boil, uncovered. Simmer for 15–20 minutes, or until the peas are very tender.

Two Strain the peas and reserve the cooking liquid. Process the peas in a food processor or blender, then return the purée to the pan. Gradually stir in the cooking liquid until you have the desired consistency.

Three Reheat the soup. Stir in the crème fraîche and adjust the seasoning. Serve immediately with croûtons and blue cheese sprinkled over.

Rillettes de porc

Pork Rillettes

- ✣ **Makes about 1.5 kg/3 lb 5 oz**
- ✣ **Prepared in 15–20 minutes**
- ✣ **Cooks in 4–6 hours**

500 g/1 lb 2 oz pork shoulder
1 kg/2 lb 4 oz pork belly, rindless and boneless
300 g/10½ oz pork fat or lard
500 ml/18 fl oz water
1 bouquet garni of 2 thyme sprigs, 2 parsley sprigs and 3 bay leaves, tied with string

1 clove
½ tsp mixed spice
grating of fresh nutmeg
salt and pepper

To serve
gherkins
mustard
baguette, sliced in half, rubbed with garlic halves and toasted

one Cut the meat into 5-cm/2-inch cubes, and chop the fat into 1-cm/½-inch cubes. Place the meat and fat in a large heavy-based saucepan with the water, bouquet garni and clove. Don't be tempted to add any more water – this method is a sort of gentle steaming.

Two Cover the pan and place it over the lowest heat your hob can create, using a heat diffuser if you've got one, or place it into a very slow oven at 120°C/250°F/Gas Mark ½. The pot should just be gently shuddering. Cook for 4–6 hours, checking and stirring about every 30 minutes to make sure that it's not burning. Remove from the heat and set aside to cool. Remove the bouquet garni and clove. While it's still slightly warm, add the spices and season to taste, then take two forks and gently tear apart the pork, mixing the fat with the meat. Be careful to keep the texture and avoid turning the meat into a paste.

three Cover the meat with a piece of greased paper or clingfilm and refrigerate for 2–3 days before serving (although you could eat it straight away). It will last for at least a further week in the refrigerator, but if you put it into sterilized jars and spread a layer of melted lard on top, it will keep for months. To serve, drop a spoonful onto a plate beside some gherkins, mustard and a baguette half.

Quiches lorraines
Quiche Lorraine Tartlets

❖ **Makes 6 quiches**
❖ **Prepared in 20–30 minutes**
❖ **Cooks in 40–50 minutes**

250 g/9 oz ready-made
  shortcrust pastry
plain flour, for dusting
125 g/4½ oz unsmoked lardons
2 large eggs
225 ml/8 fl oz whipping cream
125 g/4½ oz Gruyère cheese,
  grated
grating of fresh nutmeg
salt and pepper

one Remove the pastry from the refrigerator about 10 minutes before you roll it out and preheat the oven to 200°C/400°F/Gas Mark 6 with a baking sheet inside.

Two Divide the pastry into six equal pieces and roll out each on a lightly floured surface into 15–18-cm/6–7-inch rounds. Use to line six 12-cm/4½-inch tart tins, leaving the excess pastry hanging over the edges. Line the tart cases with greaseproof paper and fill with baking beans. Put the tart cases on the hot baking sheet and bake blind for 5 minutes, or until the rim is set. Remove the paper and beans, then return the tart cases to the oven and bake for a further 5 minutes, or until the bases look dry. Leave the tart cases on the baking sheet and remove from the oven. Reduce the oven temperature to 190°C/375°F/Gas Mark 5.

Three Meanwhile, put the lardons in a frying pan over a low heat and sauté for 3 minutes, or until the fat begins to melt. Increase the heat to medium and continue sautéeing until they are crisp.

four Sprinkle the lardons over the pastry case. Beat the eggs, cream and cheese together, then season to taste with the salt and pepper and nutmeg. Carefully divide the filling between the pastry cases, then return the tarts to the oven to bake for 20–25 minutes, or until the filling is set and the pastry is golden brown. Transfer the quiches to a wire rack to cool completely, then remove from the tins before serving.

Two

three

four

Salade niçoise
Tuna, Egg & Olive Salad

❖ Serves 4–6
❖ Prepared in 20–25 minutes
❖ Cooks in 10–15 minutes

2 tuna steaks, about 2 cm/¾ inch thick
olive oil, for brushing
250 g/9 oz French beans, trimmed

garlic vinaigrette
2 hearts of lettuce, leaves separated
3 large hard-boiled eggs, quartered
2 juicy vine-ripened tomatoes,
  cut into wedges
50 g/1¾ oz anchovy fillets in oil, drained
55 g/2 oz Niçoise olives (or black olives)
salt and pepper

one Heat a griddle pan over a high heat until you can feel the heat rising from the surface. Brush the tuna steaks with oil on one side, place oiled-side down on the hot pan and griddle for 2 minutes.

Two Lightly brush the top side of the tuna steaks with a little more oil. Use a pair of tongs to turn the tuna steaks over, then season to taste with salt and pepper. Continue griddling for a further 2 minutes for rare or up to 4 minutes for well done. Leave to cool.

Three Meanwhile, bring a saucepan of salted water to the boil. Add the beans to the pan and return to the boil, then boil for 3 minutes, or until tender but crisp. Drain the beans and immediately transfer them to a large bowl. Pour over the garlic vinaigrette and stir together, then leave the beans to cool in the dressing.

four To serve, line a platter with lettuce leaves. Lift the beans out of the bowl, leaving the excess dressing behind, and pile them in the centre of the platter. Break the tuna into large flakes and arrange it over the beans.

five Arrange the hard-boiled eggs and tomatoes around the side. Place the anchovy fillets over the salad, then scatter with the olives. Drizzle the remaining dressing in the bowl over everything and serve.

Tapenade
Olive Spread

✤ **Serves 8**
✤ **Prepared in 15–20 minutes**
✤ **No cooking**

400 g/14 oz black olives, stoned
2 tbsp capers
2 tsp Dijon mustard
juice of ½ lemon
1 garlic clove, finely chopped
12 canned anchovy fillets, drained and soaked to remove the salt
handful of chopped fresh flat-leaf parsley, plus sprigs to garnish
2 tbsp chopped fresh thyme (optional)
150 ml/5 fl oz extra virgin olive oil, plus extra for brushing
salt and pepper
rounds of baguette or ciabatta, to serve

one

one

two

one Put all the ingredients, except the salt and pepper, into a food processor and process until you get a good paste. Don't make it too smooth – it should retain a little roughness.

two Season to taste, bearing in mind that it may already be quite salty from the capers, olives and anchovies. Brush rounds of baguette with olive oil and toast the rounds.

three Serve the tapenade with the rounds of baguette and garnish with sprigs of parsley.

Soufflé au fromage
Cheese Soufflé

- ❖ Serves 4
- ❖ Prepared in 15 minutes
- ❖ Cooks in 30–35 minutes

1 tbsp butter, melted
1 tbsp finely grated Parmesan cheese
2 tbsp butter
25 g/1 oz plain flour

300 ml/10 fl oz milk
115 g/4 oz Cheddar cheese, finely grated
1 tsp wholegrain mustard
grating of fresh nutmeg
4 large eggs, separated
salt and pepper

one Preheat the oven to 200°C/400°F/Gas Mark 6. Grease the base and sides of a soufflé dish with melted butter. Then sprinkle the dish with the Parmesan cheese, turning the dish in your hands so that all the surface is covered with the cheese.

Two Melt the remaining 2 tablespoons of butter in a saucepan (preferably non-stick) over a medium heat. Add the flour, mix well using a wooden spoon and cook for 1 minute, stirring continuously. Remove from the heat and stir in the milk gradually until you have a smooth consistency.

three Return the pan to a low heat and continue to stir while the sauce comes to the boil and thickens. Simmer gently, stirring constantly, for about 3 minutes, or until the sauce is creamy and smooth. Remove from the heat and stir in the cheese, mustard and nutmeg. Season well to taste. Set aside to cool a little. Whisk the egg whites until soft peaks have formed but they are not too dry. Beat the egg yolks into the sauce mixture and then carefully stir in a little of the beaten egg white to slacken the mixture. Then carefully fold in the remaining egg whites. Turn into the prepared dish. Place on a baking sheet and cook in the preheated oven for 25–30 minutes, or until well risen and golden brown. Serve immediately.

Asperges à la sauce hollandaise
Asparagus with Hollandaise Sauce

❖ Serves 4
❖ Prepared in 10–15
   minutes
❖ Cooks in 15–20 minutes

650 g/1 lb 7 oz asparagus,
   trimmed

Hollandaise sauce
4 tbsp white wine vinegar
½ tbsp finely chopped shallots
5 black peppercorns
1 bay leaf
3 large egg yolks
140 g/5 oz unsalted butter,
   finely diced
2 tsp lemon juice
salt
pinch of cayenne pepper

one Divide the asparagus into four bundles and tie each with kitchen string, criss-crossing the string from just below the tips to the base. Stand the bundles upright in a deep saucepan. Add boiling water to come three quarters of the way up the stalks, then cover with a loose tent of foil, shiny-side down, inside the pan. Heat the water until bubbles appear around the side of the pan, then simmer for 10 minutes, or until the stalks are just tender when pierced with the tip of a knife. Drain well.

Two Meanwhile, to make the hollandaise sauce, boil the vinegar, shallots, peppercorns and bay leaf in a saucepan over a high heat until reduced to 1 tablespoon. Cool slightly, then strain into a heatproof bowl that will fit over a saucepan of simmering water.

three Beat the egg yolks into the bowl. Set the bowl over the pan of simmering water and whisk the egg yolks constantly until they are thick enough to leave a trail on the surface.

four Do not let the water boil. Gradually beat in the butter, piece by piece, whisking constantly until the sauce is like soft mayonnaise. Stir in the lemon juice, then add salt to taste and the cayenne pepper. Serve the sauce immediately with the asparagus.

one

Two

three

chapter two
Meat, Poultry & Game

Bœuf bourguignon

Steak frites

Croque-monsieur

Cassoulet

Navarin d'agneau

Gigot d'agneau aux
haricots verts

Coq au vin

Confit de canard

Bœuf bourguignon

Beef Bourguignon

✣ **Serves 6**
✣ **Prepared in 15–20 minutes**
✣ **Cooks in 3½ hours**

2 tbsp olive oil
175 g/6 oz unsmoked bacon, sliced into thin
    strips
1.3 kg/3 lb stewing beef, cut into 5-cm/2-inch
    pieces
2 carrots, sliced
2 onions, chopped
2 garlic cloves, very finely chopped

3 tbsp plain flour
700 ml/1¼ pints red wine
350–450 ml/12–16 fl oz beef stock
1 bouquet garni of 2 thyme sprigs, 2 parsley
    sprigs and 2 bay leaves, tied with string
1 tsp salt
¼ tsp pepper
3 tbsp butter
350 g/12 oz pickling onions
350 g/12 oz button mushrooms
chopped fresh flat-leaf parsley, to garnish
mashed potatoes, to serve

one Heat the oil in a large casserole over a medium heat. Add the bacon and brown for 2–3 minutes. Remove with a slotted spoon. Add the beef in batches to the casserole and cook until browned. Drain and keep with the bacon. Add the carrots and chopped onions to the casserole and cook for 5 minutes. Add the garlic and fry until just coloured. Return the meat and bacon to the casserole. Sprinkle on the flour and cook for 1 minute, stirring. Add the wine, enough stock to cover, the bouquet garni, and the salt and pepper. Bring to the boil, cover and simmer gently for 3 hours.

Two Heat half the butter in a frying pan. Add the pickling onions, cover and cook until softened. Remove with a slotted spoon and keep warm. Heat the remaining butter in the frying pan. Add the mushrooms and fry briefly. Set aside the mushrooms and keep warm.

three Remove the casserole from the heat and strain the casserole liquid through a sieve into a clean saucepan. Wipe the casserole with kitchen paper and tip in the meat mixture, mushrooms and onions. Discard the bouquet garni. Remove the surface fat from the casserole liquid, simmer for 1–2 minutes to reduce, then pour over the meat and vegetables in the casserole. Serve immediately, garnished with parsley and with mashed potatoes on the side.

Steak frites
Steak & Chips

* Serves 4
* Prepared in 20–25
  minutes
* Cooks in 45 minutes–
  1 hour

1 bunch of watercress, plus
  extra to garnish
85 g/3 oz unsalted butter,
  softened
4 sirloin steaks, about
  225 g/8 oz each
4 tsp Tabasco sauce
salt and pepper

Chips
450 g/1 lb potatoes, peeled
2 tbsp sunflower oil

one To make the chips, preheat the oven to 200°C/400°F/Gas Mark 6. Cut the potatoes into thick, even-sized chips. Rinse them under cold running water and then dry well on a clean tea towel. Place in a bowl, add the oil and toss together until coated.

two Spread the chips on a baking sheet and cook in the preheated oven for 40–45 minutes, turning once, or until golden.

three Using a sharp knife, finely chop enough watercress to fill 4 tablespoons. Place the butter in a small bowl and beat in the chopped watercress with a fork until fully incorporated. Cover with clingfilm and leave to chill in the refrigerator until required.

four Preheat a griddle pan to high. Sprinkle each steak with 1 teaspoon of the Tabasco sauce, rubbing it in well. Season to taste with salt and pepper.

five Cook the steaks on the preheated griddle for 2½ minutes each side for rare, 4 minutes each side for medium and 6 minutes each side for well done. Transfer to serving plates and serve immediately, topped with the watercress butter and accompanied by the chips. Garnish with watercress.

one

three

five

Croque-monsieur
Ham & Cheese Toastie

❖ Serves 1
❖ Prepared in 5 minutes
❖ Cooks in 5–10 minutes

2 slices white bread, buttered
2 slices smoked ham
55 g/2 oz Gruyère cheese, grated
knob of butter, melted
salt and pepper
lightly dressed mixed green salad, to serve

one Preheat the grill to high. Lay one piece of bread buttered side up and place the ham on top. Cover with two thirds of the cheese and season to taste with salt and pepper. Lay the other slice of bread on top, buttered side down. Brush the top side with the melted butter and place the bread, buttered side up, under the preheated grill.

Two Grill until browned, then remove. Turn the sandwich over and scatter the remaining cheese on top. Replace under the grill and cook until the cheese is bubbling and browned. Remove and serve with a green salad.

Cassoulet

Pork & Lamb Casserole

❖ Serves 8
❖ Prepared in 25–30
   minutes, plus soaking
❖ Cooks in 3½ hours

500 g/1 lb 2 oz dried haricot
   beans, soaked overnight
bouquet garni of 4 parsley
   sprigs, 2 thyme sprigs and
   4 bay leaves, tied with string
1 celery stick, roughly chopped
3 onions, 1 quartered, 2 thinly
   sliced
4 large garlic cloves, 2 whole,
   2 chopped
2 litres/3½ pints water
500 g/1 lb 2 oz pork belly, skin
   removed and meat cut
   into 4 large chunks
400 g/14 oz lamb shoulder,
   boned and cut into
   4 large chunks
2 tbsp duck fat or vegetable oil
400 g/14 oz Toulouse or pork
   sausage, sliced
200 g/7 oz thickly sliced bacon
2 tbsp tomato purée
150 g/5½ oz fresh breadcrumbs
salt and pepper

two

two

three

one Drain and rinse the beans and put them in a large saucepan with the bouquet garni, celery, onion quarters and whole garlic and season to taste with salt and pepper. Add the water and bring to the boil. Skim off any foam, then reduce the heat to low. Gently simmer for 1 hour, uncovered.

two Meanwhile, cut the pork and lamb into pieces 4 cm/1½ inches square, then add the duck fat to a large heavy-based saucepan and put over a high heat. Add the pork belly and brown it all over. Remove and reserve, then repeat with the sausage, then the lamb, then the bacon. Reserve the sausage, lamb and bacon. Add the sliced onions, chopped garlic and tomato purée and cook in the remaining fat for 2 minutes. Remove from the heat and leave to cool.

three Preheat the oven to 180°C/350°F/Gas Mark 4. Drain the beans, reserving the liquid but discarding the vegetables. In a large casserole, layer beans and meat alternately until they're all used up. Add the fried garlic, onion and tomato purée mixture and enough of the bean-cooking liquid to almost cover the beans. Sprinkle over the breadcrumbs and cook in the oven, covered, for 1 hour. Reduce the heat to 140°C/275°F/Gas Mark 1, remove the cover and cook for a further hour.

four Check the casserole is not too dry, adding a little heated bean liquid or water, if necessary. Serve immediately.

Navarin d'agneau
Spring Lamb Stew

❖ Serves 4–6
❖ Prepared in 15–20 minutes
❖ Cooks in 1–1¼ hours

40 g/1½ oz butter
2 tbsp sunflower oil, plus extra as needed
900 g/2 lb boned shoulder of lamb,
    trimmed and cut into large chunks,
    any bones reserved
2 shallots, finely chopped
1 tbsp sugar
1 litre/1¾ pints lamb stock

2 tbsp tomato purée
1 bouquet garni, with several parsley and
    thyme sprigs, 1 bay leaf and 1 small
    rosemary sprig
8 new potatoes, such as Charlotte,
    scrubbed and halved, if large
4 young turnips, quartered
12 baby carrots, scrubbed
140 g/5 oz frozen peas
salt and pepper
chopped fresh flat-leaf parsley, to garnish
baguette, to serve

one Melt 30 g/1 oz of the butter with the oil in a large frying pan over a medium heat.
Add the lamb, in batches to avoid overcrowding the pan, and fry, stirring, until coloured on
all sides, adding extra oil, if necessary. Transfer the meat to a large casserole as it colours.

Two Melt the remaining butter with the fat left in the pan. Add the shallots and stir
for 3 minutes, or until beginning to soften. Sprinkle with the sugar, increase the heat and
continue stirring until the shallots caramelize, taking care that they do not burn. Transfer
to the casserole and remove any charred bits from the base of the frying pan. Add half
of the stock to the pan and bring to the boil, scraping the base of the pan, then tip this
mixture into the casserole.

Three Add the remaining stock, tomato purée, bouquet garni and bones, if any, to the
casserole. Season to taste with salt and pepper. Cover and bring to the boil. Reduce the
heat and simmer for 45 minutes.

Four Add the potatoes, turnips and carrots and continue simmering for 15 minutes.
Add the peas, then uncover and simmer for a further 5–10 minutes, or until the meat
and all the vegetables are tender. Remove and discard the bones, if used, and the bouquet
garni. Taste and adjust the seasoning, if necessary. Garnish with parsley and serve with a
baguette for soaking up the juices.

Gigot d'agneau aux haricots verts
Roast Leg of Lamb with French Beans

✤ Serves 4–6
✤ Prepared in 10 minutes, plus marinating and resting
✤ Cooks in 1–1½ hours

3 garlic cloves, thinly sliced
1 leg of lamb portion (preferably salt marsh lamb), about 1.3 kg/3 lb
olive oil, for rubbing
125 ml/4 fl oz dry red wine
125 ml/4 fl oz water
2 tbsp capers in brine, rinsed
280 g/10 oz French beans, trimmed
30 g/1 oz butter
salt and pepper

one Make deep incisions all over the lamb and push a slice of garlic into each of the slits. Rub the leg all over with salt and pepper. Place in a roasting tin, rub all over with oil and set aside for at least 1 hour.

Two Meanwhile, preheat the oven to 230°C/450°F/Gas Mark 8. Calculate the roasting time at 15 minutes per 500 g/1 lb 2 oz plus 15 minutes for medium, and 20 minutes per 500 g/1 lb 2 oz plus 20 minutes for well done.

three Roast the lamb in the preheated oven for 10 minutes, then reduce the oven temperature to 180°C/350°F/Gas Mark 4 and continue roasting for the calculated roasting time. Transfer the lamb to a carving dish, cover with a sheet of foil and leave to rest for 20 minutes.

four While the lamb is resting, pour off any excess fat from the tin. Add the wine and water to the juices remaining in the tin and bring to the boil, scraping the sediment from base of the tin. Add the capers and heat through. Season this gravy to taste with salt and pepper.

five Ten minutes before serving, bring a saucepan of lightly salted water to the boil. Add the beans, bring back to the boil and cook for 5–8 minutes, or until tender. Drain well and return to the pan. Add the butter and season to taste with salt and pepper.

six Carve the lamb and serve immediately with the French beans, alongside the gravy for spooning over.

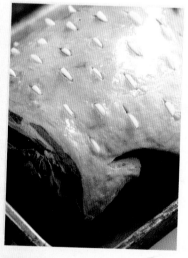

one

four

five

Coq au vin
Chicken in Wine

❖ **Serves 4**
❖ **Prepared in 15–20 minutes**
❖ **Cooks in 1½ hours**

55 g/2 oz butter
2 tbsp olive oil
1.8 kg/4 lb skinless, boneless chicken breasts
115 g/4 oz rindless smoked bacon,
  cut into strips
115 g/4 oz baby onions

115 g/4 oz chestnut mushrooms, halved
2 garlic cloves, finely chopped
2 tbsp brandy
225 ml/8 fl oz red wine
300 ml/10 fl oz chicken stock
bouquet garni sachet
2 tbsp plain flour
salt and pepper
bay leaves, to garnish

one Melt half of the butter with the olive oil in a large casserole. Add the chicken and cook over a medium heat, stirring, for 8–10 minutes, or until golden brown all over. Add the bacon, onions, mushrooms and garlic.

Two Pour in the brandy and set alight with a match. When the flames have died down, add the wine, stock and bouquet garni and season to taste with salt and pepper. Bring to the boil, reduce the heat and simmer gently for 1 hour, or until the chicken breasts are cooked through and the juices run clear when a skewer is inserted into the thickest part of the meat. Meanwhile, make a beurre manié by mashing the remaining butter with the flour in a bowl.

Three Discard the bouquet garni. Transfer the chicken to a large plate using a slotted spoon and keep warm. Slowly stir the beurre manié into the casserole. Bring to the boil, return the chicken to the casserole and serve immediately, garnished with bay leaves.

Confit de canard

Duck Confit

+ Serves 4
+ Prepared in 5 minutes, plus chilling and maturing
+ Cooks in 3–4 hours

4 duck legs, about 280 g/10 oz each
4 tbsp coarse sea salt
1 tsp pepper
6 fresh thyme sprigs, chopped
4 fresh rosemary sprigs, chopped
2 bay leaves
1–1.25 kg/2 lb 4 oz–2 lb 12 oz duck fat, goose fat or lard, plus extra, if necessary
Sautéed Potatoes and green salad, to serve

one Prepare the duck legs at least 8 days before you intend to serve them – they will be stored in airtight, heatproof, non-metallic containers until needed. Rub each duck leg with the salt, then put them in the container or containers. Sprinkle with the pepper, thyme and rosemary and tuck in the bay leaves. Cover tightly and refrigerate for at least 24 hours or for up to 48 hours.

two To cook, preheat the oven to 120°C/250°F/Gas Mark ½. Wipe the duck legs and discard the accumulated moisture and flavourings. Place the duck legs in a large casserole. Add the fat and heat until it melts. Cover the casserole and transfer it to the oven for 3–4 hours, or until the duck legs have rendered their fat and are very tender.

three Remove the legs and set aside. Strain the fat through a fine sieve. Pour a layer of the fat in the bottom of the container or containers and leave to set. Add the duck legs and pour over enough fat to cover them by at least 2.5 cm/1 inch.

four Leave the duck legs and fat to cool, then cover and refrigerate for at least 1 week before using. When ready to use, place the container in simmering water to melt the fat. At this point the duck legs can be used in other recipes or fried to serve with a salad. To fry, heat 2 tablespoons of the fat in a frying pan over a medium-high heat. Fry the duck legs, skin side down, for 4–5 minutes, or until the skin browns. Turn them over and fry on the other side for a further 2 minutes. Serve immediately, with the potatoes and salad.

BRASSERIE DE LA CANCHE

Fish & Seafood

tartare de saumon

Salmon Tartare

- ✤ Serves 4
- ✤ Prepared in 25–30 minutes, plus chilling
- ✤ No cooking

500 g/1 lb 2 oz salmon fillet, skinned
2 tbsp sea salt
1 tbsp caster sugar
2 tbsp chopped fresh dill
1 tbsp chopped fresh tarragon
1 tsp Dijon mustard
juice of 1 lemon
salt and pepper

Topping
400 g/14 oz cream cheese
1 tbsp chopped fresh chives
pinch of paprika
snipped fresh dill and chives, to garnish

one

Two

three

one Put the salmon into a shallow baking dish. Combine the sea salt, sugar and dill, then rub the mixture into the fish until well coated. Season with plenty of pepper. Cover with clingfilm and refrigerate for at least 48 hours, turning the salmon once.

Two When ready to serve, put the chopped tarragon into a mixing bowl with the mustard and lemon juice. Season well. Remove the salmon from the refrigerator, chop into small pieces then add to the bowl. Stir until the salmon is well coated.

three To make the topping, put the cream cheese, chives and paprika into a separate bowl and mix well. Place a 10-cm/4-inch steel cooking ring or round biscuit cutter on each of four small serving plates. Divide the salmon between the four steel rings so that each ring is half full. Level the surface of each one, then top with the cream cheese mixture. Smooth the surfaces, then carefully remove the steel rings. Garnish with fresh dill and chives and serve immediately.

Sole meunière

Butter-fried Sole

❖ Serves 2
❖ Prepared in 15–20 minutes
❖ Cooks in 15–20 minutes

4 sole fillets, each about 175 g/6 oz,
  skinned
100 ml/3½ fl oz milk

4 tbsp plain flour
85 g/3 oz butter
juice of ½ lemon
salt and pepper
chopped fresh flat-leaf parsley, to garnish
cooked asparagus and lemon
  wedges, to serve

one Rinse the fish under cold running water and pat dry with kitchen paper. Pour the milk into a flat dish at least as large as the fillets and put the flour on a plate. Season each fillet on both sides with salt and pepper to taste.

Two Working with one fillet at a time, pull it very quickly through the milk, then put it in the flour, turn once to coat all over and shake off any excess flour. Continue until all the fillets are prepared.

Three Melt half the butter in a sauté pan or frying pan, large enough to hold the fillets in a single layer, over a medium-high heat. Add the fillets to the pan, skinned-side down, and fry for 2 minutes.

four Turn over the fillets and fry for 2–3 minutes, or until the flesh flakes easily. Transfer to warmed serving plates, skinned-side up, and set aside.

five Reduce the heat to medium and melt the remaining butter in the pan. When it stops foaming, add the lemon juice and stir, scraping the sediment from the base of the pan. Spoon the butter mixture over the fish and garnish with parsley. Serve with asparagus and lemon wedges.

Tuna Steaks

❖ Serves 4
❖ Prepared in 10 minutes, plus chilling
❖ Cooks in 3–4½ minutes

4 tuna steaks, each about
  4 cm/1½ inch thick, at room
  temperature
olive oil, for brushing
salt and pepper
mixed salad leaves, to serve

Mediterranean butter
1 garlic clove, finely chopped
125 g/4½ oz butter, softened
2 tbsp chopped fresh dill
4 black olives in brine, drained,
  stoned and very finely
  chopped
2 anchovy fillets in oil, drained
  and very finely chopped
2 sun-dried tomatoes in oil,
  drained and very finely
  chopped
finely grated rind of 1 lemon
pinch of cayenne pepper,
  or to taste
salt and pepper

one

Two

Three

one At least 3 hours before you plan to cook, make the butter. Put the garlic clove on a chopping board and sprinkle with salt. Use the flat side of a knife to crush and scrape the garlic until a paste forms. Beat the garlic, butter, dill, olives, anchovies, sun-dried tomatoes, lemon rind and cayenne pepper together in a bowl until all the ingredients are mixed. Season to taste with salt and pepper.

Two Scrape the butter mixture on to a piece of greaseproof paper and roll into a short log about 2.5 cm/1 inch thick. Twist the ends of the paper to make a compact shape, then cut off any excess paper from one end. Stand the butter log upright in a glass and chill for at least 3 hours.

Three Heat a large griddle pan over a high heat. Brush the tuna with oil and season with salt and pepper on both sides. Place the tuna steaks in the pan and griddle for 2 minutes. Brush the tuna with a little more oil, turn the steaks over and continue cooking for a further 1 minute for medium-rare or up to 2½ minutes for well done. Transfer the tuna steaks to plates and top each with a slice of the chilled butter. Serve immediately, with mixed salad leaves.

Pan-fried Sea Bass

- ♣ Serves 4
- ♣ Prepared in 20–25 minutes
- ♣ Cooks in 35–40 minutes

800 g/1 lb 12 oz large potatoes, cut into chunks
6 whole garlic cloves, unpeeled
200 ml/7 fl oz milk

100 ml/3½ fl oz double cream
55 g/2 oz butter, diced
4 x 200 g/7 oz sea bass fillets,
    scaled but not skinned
3 tbsp olive oil
salt and pepper
peas and lemon wedges, to serve

one Fill a large saucepan with cold water, add some salt and the potatoes and bring to the boil. Simmer the potatoes for 10–15 minutes, or until tender, then drain and return to the pan. Heat and stir for a further 2 minutes to dry them out. Mash them using a potato ricer and set aside in the warm pan.

Two Bring a small saucepan of water to the boil, add the garlic and blanch for 2 minutes, then drain and run under a little cold water. Peel off the skins and mash the garlic using a garlic crusher or the back of a spoon. Mix this into the potato. Put the milk in a saucepan and heat until hot but not boiling, then stir it into the potato, along with the cream. Heat this over a low heat for about 5 minutes, adding the butter a cube at a time. The potato should have a smooth consistency like a thick mayonnaise. Cover and keep warm.

Three Carefully score the skin of the fish with a few diagonal cuts, taking care not to cut the flesh. Season with salt and pepper. Pour the oil into a large frying pan and place over a medium-high heat until shimmering. Fry the fillets, skin-side down, for 4 minutes. Check that the skin is crispy, then turn very carefully and fry on the other side for just 1 minute. Spread some potato in the centre of four warmed plates and place a fish fillet on top, skin side up. Serve with peas and lemon wedges.

Bouillinade

Fish & Potato Stew

❖ Serves 4
❖ Prepared in 5 minutes
❖ Cooks in 30–45 minutes

1½ tbsp olive oil, plus extra for
   brushing
1 onion, finely chopped
3 large garlic cloves,
   2 chopped and 1 halved
1 tbsp fennel seeds
½ tsp dried chilli flakes,
   or to taste
pinch of saffron threads
400 g/14 oz canned chopped
   tomatoes
125 ml/4 fl oz fish stock or
   water
2 bay leaves
500 g/1 lb 2 oz floury potatoes,
   thinly sliced
900 g/2 lb mixed fish, such
   as hake, monkfish and red
   snapper, skinned and cut into
   chunks
2 red peppers, deseeded and
   sliced
2 tbsp chopped fresh flat-leaf
   parsley
salt and pepper

one Preheat the oven to 180°C/350°F/Gas Mark 4.

Two Heat the oil in a saucepan over a medium heat. Add the onion and fry, stirring, for 2 minutes. Add the chopped garlic, fennel seeds, chilli flakes and saffron and continue frying for a further 1 minute, or until the onion is soft. Add the tomatoes, stock and bay leaves and season to taste with salt and pepper. Cover and bring to the boil, then reduce the heat to very low and simmer for 10 minutes. Taste and adjust the seasoning, if necessary.

three Meanwhile, rub the garlic halves all over a 1.5-litre/2¾-pint baking dish, pressing down firmly, then set aside the dish, discarding the garlic. Bring a large saucepan of lightly salted water to the boil, add the potatoes, bring back to the boil and cook for 8–10 minutes, or until they are starting to soften but still hold their shape. Drain well, pat dry and set aside.

four Place the prepared dish on a baking sheet and arrange half the potatoes in a layer at the bottom of the dish. Place the fish and red peppers on top. Spoon over the tomato sauce, sprinkle with the parsley and shake the dish slightly. Arrange the remaining potatoes on top to cover all the other ingredients and lightly brush with oil. Bake in the preheated oven for 20–25 minutes, or until the fish and potatoes are tender when pierced with a skewer. Serve immediately.

Two

three

four

Moules marinières
Mussels in Wine

✤ Serves 4
✤ Prepared in 10–15 minutes
✤ Cooks in 8–10 minutes

2 kg/4 lb 8 oz live mussels, scrubbed and
  debearded
300 ml/10 fl oz dry white wine
6 shallots, finely chopped
bouquet garni sachet
pepper
fresh flat-leaf parsley sprigs,
  to garnish
baguette, to serve

one Discard any mussels with broken shells and any that refuse to close when tapped.

Two Pour the wine into a large heavy-based saucepan, add the shallots and bouquet garni and season to taste with pepper. Bring to the boil over a medium heat, add the mussels and cover tightly. Cook, shaking the saucepan occasionally, for 3–4 minutes, or until the mussels have opened. Remove and discard the bouquet garni and any mussels that remain closed.

Three Using a slotted spoon, divide the mussels among individual serving dishes. Tilt the saucepan to let any sand settle, then spoon the cooking liquid over the mussels. Garnish with parsley sprigs and serve immediately with baguette.

Crevettes à la grecque

Prawns in Mediterranean Sauce

❖ Serves 4
❖ Prepared in
    12–15 minutes, plus
    cooling and chilling
❖ Cooks in 30 minutes

125 ml/4 fl oz dry white wine
125 ml/4 fl oz water
6 tbsp olive oil
2 large garlic cloves,
    thinly sliced
1 small red onion,
    finely chopped
thinly pared zest of
    1 large lemon
2 tbsp lemon juice
1 tbsp coriander seeds,
    toasted and lightly crushed
½ tbsp black or pink
    peppercorns, lightly crushed
pinch of dried chilli flakes,
    or to taste
20 raw tiger prawns, peeled
    and deveined
salt and pepper
chopped fresh flat-leaf parsley,
    dill or coriander, to garnish
sliced baguette, to serve

one

two

three

one Put the wine, water, oil, garlic, onion, lemon zest and juice, coriander seeds, peppercorns and chilli flakes into a saucepan. Cover and bring to the boil over a high heat, then reduce the heat and simmer for 20 minutes.

Two Add the prawns to the liquid and simmer for 2–3 minutes, or until they turn pink. Use a slotted spoon to remove the prawns from the liquid immediately and transfer them to a deep bowl.

Three Bring the poaching liquid back to the boil, uncovered, and boil for 5 minutes, or until reduced by half. Leave to cool to lukewarm, then pour over the prawns. Season the prawns to taste with salt and pepper and leave to cool completely. Cover the bowl with clingfilm and chill for at least 4 hours.

four When ready to serve, garnish with parsley and serve chilled, with plenty of sliced baguette for mopping up the juices.

Bouillabaisse

Seafood Stew

❖ Serves 8
❖ Prepared in 20–25 minutes
❖ Cooks in 50–55 minutes

1 kg/2 lb 4 oz selection of at least 4 different
   firm white fish fillets, such as red mullet,
   snapper, sea bass, eel or monkfish, scaled
   and cleaned, but not skinned
100 ml/3½ fl oz olive oil
2 onions, finely chopped
1 fennel bulb, finely chopped
4 garlic cloves, crushed
1.25 kg/2 lb 12 oz canned chopped
   tomatoes
1.5 litres/2¾ pints fish stock

pinch of saffron strands
grated zest of 1 orange
bouquet garni of 2 thyme sprigs, 2 parsley
   sprigs and 2 bay leaves, tied together with
   string
500 g/1 lb 2 oz live mussels, scrubbed and
   debearded
500 g/1 lb 2 oz cooked prawns, shell on
salt and pepper
baguette, to serve

one Carefully pin-bone the fish, then cut the fillets into bite-sized pieces. Heat the olive oil in a very large frying pan or wide saucepan with a lid and gently fry the onion and fennel for about 15 minutes, or until soft. Add the garlic and fry for 2 minutes, then add the tomatoes and simmer for 2 minutes. Add the stock, saffron, orange zest and bouquet garni and bring to the boil. Simmer, uncovered, for 15 minutes.

Two Discard any mussels with broken shells and any that refuse to close when tapped. Add the fish pieces, mussels and prawns and cover the pan. Simmer for a further 5–10 minutes, or until the mussels have opened. Discard any that remain closed. Season to taste with salt and pepper.

Three Serve immediately with some crusty baguette.

59

Vegetable Dishes

Ratatouille
Roasted Vegetables in Sauce

✤ **Serves 4**
✤ **Prepared in 20–25 minutes**
✤ **Cooks in 1½ hours**

3 red peppers
200 ml/7 fl oz olive oil
250 g/9 oz courgettes, thickly sliced
1 fennel bulb, roughly chopped
2 large red onions, roughly sliced

3 white onions, thickly sliced
2 large aubergines, thickly sliced
600 g/1 lb 5 oz ripe tomatoes, blanched, peeled, cored and deseeded
1 large tbsp fresh thyme leaves
1 large tbsp fresh rosemary leaves
1 tsp sugar
salt and pepper
crusty bread, to serve (optional)

one Preheat the grill to high, then place the red peppers on the grill tray and place under the heat until the skin blackens. Turn and grill again, continuing until they are blackened all over. Put them in a bowl and cover with clingfilm to sweat for 10 minutes, then peel them under cold running water. Cut them open and deseed them, then chop the flesh into large chunks.

Two Meanwhile, place a large heavy-based saucepan over a medium heat and add half of the oil. Add the courgettes and fry until they begin to brown. Transfer them to a large roasting tin and keep warm. Add the fennel and onions to the pan and fry for 15–20 minutes until they soften, then transfer them to the roasting tin. Add the aubergines and some more oil (they will soak up a lot) to the pan and fry until they begin to brown. Add them to the roasting tin, laid flat in a single layer.

three Preheat the oven to 190°C/375°F/Gas Mark 5. Add the tomatoes, red peppers, thyme and rosemary to the roasting tin and distribute the vegetables evenly across it. Sprinkle the sugar over the whole lot and gently mix through. There should be one layer of vegetables, not a stew – if you need more room, use two roasting tins. Season with salt and pepper, drizzle with olive oil and place, uncovered, in the preheated oven for 40–50 minutes, or until they start to brown.

four Refrigerate overnight or serve immediately with crusty bread, if using.

Gratin de courgettes

Courgette & Cheese Gratin

✤ Serves 4–6
✤ Prepared in 25–30 minutes
✤ Cooks in 50–55 minutes

55 g/2 oz butter, plus extra for greasing
6 courgettes, sliced
2 tbsp chopped fresh tarragon or a mixture of fresh mint, tarragon and flat-leaf parsley
200 g/7 oz Gruyère or Parmesan cheese, grated
125 ml/4 fl oz milk
125 ml/4 fl oz double cream
2 eggs, beaten
freshly grated nutmeg
salt and pepper

two

three

four

one Preheat the oven to 180°C/350°F/Gas Mark 4.
Grease a large baking dish.

Two Melt the butter in a large sauté or frying pan over
a medium-high heat. Add the courgettes and sauté for
4–6 minutes, turning the slices over occasionally, until
coloured on both sides. Remove from the pan and drain on
kitchen paper, then season to taste with salt and pepper.

Three Spread half the courgettes over the base of the prepared
dish. Sprinkle with half of the herbs and 85 g/3 oz of the cheese. Repeat
these layers once more.

four Mix the milk, cream and eggs together in a jug and add nutmeg and salt and
pepper to taste. Pour this liquid over the courgettes, then sprinkle the top with the
remaining cheese.

five Bake in the preheated oven for 35–45 minutes, or until it is set in the centre
and golden brown. Remove from the oven and leave to stand for 5 minutes before
serving straight from the dish.

Tarte à l'oignon

French Onion Tart

❖ **Serves 4**
❖ **Prepared in 20–25 minutes, plus chilling**
❖ **Cooks in 1¼ hours**

Pastry
200 g/7 oz plain flour, plus extra for dusting
pinch of salt
100 g/3½ oz butter, plus extra for greasing
1 egg yolk

Filling
75 g/2¾ oz butter
4 onions, thinly sliced
2 tsp thyme leaves
2 eggs
225 ml/8 fl oz double cream
50 g/1¾ oz Gruyère cheese, grated
½ tsp fresh grated nutmeg
salt and pepper

one First, make the pastry. Sift the flour and salt together into a large bowl, dice the butter and add to the bowl, then rub with your fingers until the mixture resembles fine breadcrumbs. Add the egg yolk and just enough water to bind to a soft, but not sticky, dough. Roll into a ball, wrap in clingfilm and refrigerate for 15 minutes before using.

Two Preheat the oven to 180°C/350°F/Gas Mark 4. Roll out the pastry on a lightly floured surface. Press the pastry into a greased 20-cm/8-inch loose-based tart tin, lay a piece of baking paper on it, cover with baking beans and bake blind in the preheated oven for 15 minutes. Remove from the oven and increase the oven temperature to 200°C/400°F/Gas Mark 6. Remove the beans and paper and bake the pastry case for a further 5 minutes. Leave the oven on.

three To make the filling, melt the butter in a large, heavy-based frying pan over a low-medium heat, then add the onions and thyme and fry gently, stirring frequently until lightly browned. This will take 15–30 minutes. Season with salt and pepper, remove from the heat and leave to cool for 10 minutes.

four Lower the oven temperature to 190°C/375°F/Gas Mark 5. In a large bowl, beat the eggs and cream together. Add the cheese, nutmeg and cooked onion mixture and stir. Pour the mixture into the pastry case and bake, uncovered, for 30–40 minutes, or until golden brown. Serve immediately.

Tarte aux tomates

Tomato Tart

❖ **Serves 4**
❖ **Prepared in 20–25 minutes**
❖ **Cooks in 40–45 minutes**

Pastry
250 g/9 oz plain flour
pinch of salt
140 g/5 oz butter
1 tbsp chopped oregano,
    plus extra to garnish
5–6 tbsp cold water

Filling
25 g/1 oz butter
1 tbsp caster sugar
500 g/1 lb 2 oz tomatoes, halved
1 garlic clove, crushed
2 tsp white wine vinegar
salt and pepper

one

three

three

one Preheat the oven to 200°C/400°F/Gas Mark 6. To make the filling, melt the butter in a heavy-based saucepan. Add the sugar and stir over a fairly high heat until just turning golden brown. Remove from the heat and quickly add the tomatoes, garlic and white wine vinegar, stirring to coat evenly. Season with salt and pepper.

Two Tip the tomatoes into a 23-cm/9-inch cake tin and arrange cut-side down.

three To make the pastry, place the flour, salt, butter and oregano in a food processor and process until the mixture resembles fine breadcrumbs. Add just enough water to bind to a soft, but not sticky, dough. Roll out the pastry to a 25-cm/10-inch round and place over the tomatoes, tucking in the edges. Pierce with a fork to let out steam.

four Bake in the preheated oven for 25–30 minutes, or until firm and golden. Rest for 2–3 minutes, then run a knife around the edge and turn out onto a warmed serving plate.

five Sprinkle the tart with chopped oregano, and serve immediately.

Aumonières de poireaux

Leek Crêpes

❖ **Makes 8**
❖ **Prepared in 20–25 minutes**
❖ **Cooks in 35 minutes**

Filling
30 g/1 oz unsalted butter
½ tbsp sunflower oil
200 g/7 oz leeks, finely shredded
freshly grated nutmeg, to taste
1 tbsp finely snipped fresh chives
85 g/3 oz soft goat's cheese,
   rind removed if necessary, chopped
salt and pepper

Savoury crêpes
150 g/5½ oz plain flour
pinch of salt
250 ml/9 fl oz milk
1 large egg
2 tbsp melted butter
butter, for frying

one Preheat the oven to 200°C/400°F/Gas Mark 6. To make the filling, melt the butter with the oil in a frying pan with a lid over a medium-high heat. Add the leeks and stir so that they are well coated. Stir in salt and pepper to taste, but remember the cheese might be salty. Add a few gratings of nutmeg, then cover the leeks with a sheet of wet greaseproof paper and put the lid on the pan. Reduce the heat to very low and leave the leeks to sweat for 5–7 minutes, or until tender but not brown. Stir in the chives, then season to taste.

Two To make the crêpes, sift the flour and salt into a bowl. Add the milk, egg and melted butter and whisk to a smooth batter. Leave to stand for 15 minutes. Heat the butter in a large frying pan. Pour in just enough batter to cover the pan, swirling to create a thin layer. Cook until the underside is golden, then flip and cook the other side. Repeat with the remaining batter until you have eight crêpes.

three Put one crêpe on the work surface and put one eighth of the leeks on the crêpe, top with one eighth of the cheese, then fold the crêpe into a square parcel or simply roll it around the filling. Place the stuffed crêpe on a baking sheet, then continue to fill and fold or roll the remaining crêpes. Put the baking sheet in the preheated oven and bake for 5 minutes, or until the crêpes are hot and the cheese starts to melt. Serve immediately.

Clafoutis au fromage
Cheese Bake

✤ Serves 4–6
✤ Prepared in 15 minutes
✣ Cooks in 50–55 minutes

olive oil, for greasing
450 g/1 lb cherry tomatoes
85 g/3 oz goat's cheese, rind
    removed if necessary, finely
    crumbled
2 tbsp fresh thyme leaves
55 g/2 oz plain flour
pinch of sugar
4 large eggs
300 ml/10 fl oz milk
salt
mixed salad leaves, dressed
    with garlic vinaigrette, to
    serve (optional)

one

two

three

one Preheat the oven to 180°C/350°F/Gas Mark 4. Lightly grease a 1.5-litre/2¾-pint baking dish. Arrange the tomatoes in a single layer in the dish, then scatter over the cheese and thyme and set aside.

two Sift the flour, sugar and a pinch of salt into a large bowl and make a well in the centre. Break the eggs into the well and use a whisk or fork to blend them together. Add half the milk and stir, gradually incorporating the flour from the side of the bowl, until blended. Stir in the remaining milk until a smooth batter forms.

three Gently pour the batter over the tomatoes, shaking the dish slightly to distribute the cheese and thyme. Place in the preheated oven and bake for 50–55 minutes, or until the batter is puffed, golden and set and the tomatoes are tender.

four Remove the clafoutis from the oven and leave to stand for 5 minutes before serving. Alternatively, leave to cool completely and then serve with a dressed salad, if using.

Artichauts entiers
Whole Artichokes

✤ Serves 4
✤ Prepared in 20–25 minutes, plus
  cooling
✤ Cooks in 40–45 minutes

2 lemons
4 large globe artichokes
250 g/9 oz butter
2 tbsp fresh thyme leaves
zest and juice of 1 lemon
salt and pepper
crusty bread, to serve

one Half fill a large saucepan with cold water. Halve the lemons, squeeze the juice into the water and drop the skins in too. Cut the stalks off the artichokes near the base, then 'scalp' them by chopping off the top 2.5 cm/1 inch of the leaves. Add them to the water, cover and bring to the boil. Once boiling, the artichokes will take 20–30 minutes to cook, depending on their tenderness and size. They are ready when the outer leaves can be pulled off without any effort.

two Drain the artichokes, turn them upside down and leave to cool for 15 minutes while you make the lemon and thyme-flavoured butter. Gently melt the butter in a small saucepan, and mix in the thyme, lemon zest and juice and salt and pepper.

three Place the artichokes in four shallow bowls and season to taste with salt and pepper. Serve the butter with the artichokes, in four small bowls or in the removed outer leaves of the artichoke. Place a large bowl in the middle of the table for discarded artichoke bits and leaves.

Omelette aux fines herbes
Mixed Herb Omelette

✤ Serves 1
✤ Prepared in 10 minutes
✤ Cooks in 15–20 minutes

2 large eggs
2 tbsp milk
40 g/1½ oz butter
leaves from 1 fresh flat-leaf
   parsley sprig, plus extra
   to garnish
1 fresh chervil sprig, chopped,
   plus extra to garnish
2 fresh chives, snipped, plus
   extra to garnish
salt and pepper

one Break the eggs into a bowl. Add the milk and salt and pepper to taste, and quickly beat until just blended.

two Heat a 20-cm/8-inch omelette pan or frying pan over a medium-high heat until it is very hot and you can feel the heat rising from the surface. Add 30 g/1 oz of the butter and use a fork to rub it over the base and around the sides as it melts.

three As soon as the butter stops sizzling, pour in the eggs. Shake the pan forwards and backwards over the heat and use the fork to stir the eggs around the pan in a circular motion. Do not scrape the base of the pan.

four As the omelette begins to set, use the fork to push the cooked egg from the edge towards the centre, so the remaining uncooked egg comes in contact with the hot base of the pan. Continue doing this for 3 minutes, or until the omelette looks set on the bottom, but is still slightly runny on top.

five Place the herbs in the centre of the omelette. Tilt the pan away from the handle, so the omelette slides towards the edge of the pan. Use the fork to fold the top part of the omelette over the herbs and then fold over the bottom part. Slide the omelette onto a plate, then rub the remaining butter over the top. Serve immediately.

one

four

five

chapter five

Desserts

Crème brûlée
Crème brûlée

* ❖ Serves 6
* ❖ Prepared in 20–25 minutes
* ❖ Cooks in 1 hour

500 ml/18 fl oz double cream
1 vanilla pod
100 g/3½ oz caster sugar, plus extra
  for the topping
6 egg yolks

one Preheat the oven to 160°C/325°F/Gas Mark 3.

Two Pour the cream into a small saucepan. Split the vanilla pod in half lengthways. Scrape the seeds into the pan, then chop the pod into little pieces and add that too. Heat the cream to boiling, then reduce the heat and simmer gently for 5 minutes.

three Put the sugar and egg yolks in a heatproof bowl and beat with a spoon until well mixed. Pour the hot cream into the egg mixture, beating (not whisking) as you pour, until it's nicely thickened. Pass this custard through a fine sieve into another bowl or jug. Pour the mixture into a wide, flat dish and lay this in a roasting tray. Boil a kettle and carefully pour the hot water into the tray so that it comes halfway up the sides of the crème brûlée dish.

four Place in the preheated oven and bake for about 30–45 minutes, or until the custard has just set.

five Remove from the oven and leave to cool to room temperature. Sprinkle some caster sugar over the custard and then gently caramelize it using a kitchen blow torch, or under a very hot grill. Leave to cool for a few minutes then serve.

Tarte Tatin
Apple Tart

✤ **Serves 6**
✤ **Prepared in 25–30 minutes,**
   plus resting
✤ **Cooks in 45–50 minutes**

200 g/7 oz caster sugar
150 g/5½ oz unsalted butter
800 g/1 lb 12 oz Cox or Golden Delicious
   apples, peeled, cored and sliced
350 g/12 oz ready-made puff pastry
plain flour, for dusting
vanilla ice cream, to serve (optional)

one Place a 20-cm/8-inch ovenproof frying pan over a low heat and add the sugar. Melt the sugar until it starts to caramelize, but do not let it burn, then add the butter and stir it in to make a light toffee sauce. Remove from the heat.

two Place the apple slices in the pan on top of the toffee sauce. The apples should fill the pan. Put the pan over a medium heat and cover. Simmer, without stirring, for about 5–10 minutes, or until the apples have soaked up some of the sauce, then remove from the heat.

three Preheat the oven to 190°C/375°F/Gas Mark 5. Roll out the pastry on a lightly floured surface until the pastry is large enough to thickly cover the pan, with extra space on the sides. Lay it on top of the apples and tuck the edges down inside between the fruit and the pan until it is sealed. Don't worry about making it look too neat – it will be turned over before eating.

four Put the pan into the preheated oven and bake for 25–35 minutes, checking to make sure the pastry doesn't burn. The pastry should be puffed and golden. Remove from the oven and leave to rest for 30–60 minutes.

five When you're ready to eat, make sure the tart is still a little warm (reheat it on the hob, if necessary) and place a plate on top. Carefully turn it over and lift the frying pan off. Serve with some vanilla ice cream, if using.

Macarons à la vanille
Vanilla Macaroons

❖ **Makes 16**
❖ **Prepared in 30 minutes,
  plus resting**
❖ **Cooks in 10–15 minutes**

75 g/2¾ oz ground almonds
115 g/4 oz icing sugar
2 large egg whites
50 g/1¾ oz caster sugar
½ tsp vanilla extract

Filling
55 g/2 oz unsalted butter,
  softened
½ tsp vanilla extract
115 g/4 oz icing sugar, sifted

three

four

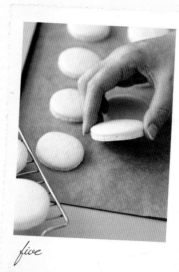

five

one Place the ground almonds and icing sugar in a food processor and process for 15 seconds. Sift the mixture into a bowl. Line two baking sheets with baking paper.

two Place the egg whites in a large bowl and whisk until holding soft peaks. Gradually whisk in the caster sugar to make a firm, glossy meringue. Whisk in the vanilla extract.

three Using a spatula, fold the almond mixture into the meringue one third at a time. When all the dry ingredients are thoroughly incorporated, continue to cut and fold the mixture until it forms a shiny batter with a thick, ribbon-like consistency.

four Pour the mixture into a piping bag fitted with a 1-cm/½-inch plain nozzle. Pipe 32 small rounds onto the prepared baking sheets. Tap the baking sheets firmly onto a work surface to remove air bubbles. Leave at room temperature for 30 minutes. Preheat the oven to 160°C/325°F/Gas Mark 3.

five Bake in the preheated oven for 10–15 minutes. Cool for 10 minutes, then carefully peel the macaroons off the baking paper. Leave to cool completely.

six To make the filling, beat the butter and vanilla extract in a bowl until pale and fluffy. Gradually beat in the icing sugar until smooth and creamy. Use to sandwich pairs of macaroons together.

Clafoutis aux myrtilles
Blueberry Bake

* ❖ Serves 4
* ❖ Prepared in 15–20 minutes
* ❖ Cooks in 30 minutes

25 g/1 oz butter, softened,
   plus extra for greasing
125 g/4½ oz caster sugar
3 eggs
60 g/2¼ oz plain flour
250 ml/9 fl oz single cream
½ tsp ground cinnamon
450 g/1 lb blueberries
icing sugar, for dusting
single cream, to serve (optional)

one Preheat the oven to 180°C/350°F/Gas Mark 4. Grease a 1-litre/1¾-pint baking dish.

two Put the butter in a bowl with the caster sugar and beat together until pale and creamy. Add the eggs and beat together well. Sift in the flour, then gradually stir in the cream followed by the cinnamon. Continue to stir until smooth.

three Arrange the blueberries in the base of the prepared baking dish, then pour over the batter. Transfer to the preheated oven and bake for about 30 minutes, or until puffed and golden.

four Remove from the oven, dust lightly with icing sugar and serve with cream, if using.

Parfait à la framboise
Raspberry Parfait

✤ Serves 6
✤ Prepared in 15 minutes,
   plus freezing
✤ Cooks in 10 minutes

450 g/1 lb raspberries, plus
   extra to decorate
85 g/3 oz icing sugar
1 tbsp kirsch or cherry brandy
   (optional)
75 g/2¾ oz granulated sugar
125 ml/4 fl oz water
2 egg whites
300 ml/10 fl oz whipping cream

one Put the raspberries in a food processor or blender and process to form a smooth purée. Push through a nylon sieve into a bowl to remove the seeds.

Two Sift the icing sugar into the raspberry purée, then stir together until well mixed. Stir in the kirsch or cherry brandy, if using.

three Put the granulated sugar and water in a small heavy-based saucepan over a low heat and heat gently, stirring, until the sugar has dissolved. Bring to the boil, then boil, without stirring, for 5 minutes, or until a syrup has formed. Do not allow it to brown. Meanwhile, whisk the egg whites in a large bowl until stiff and dry.

four Drizzle the hot sugar syrup in a thin stream onto the whisked egg whites, whisking all the time until the mixture is thick, creamy and fluffy. Continue whisking until the mixture is cold.

five Whip the cream until stiff. Fold the raspberry purée into the egg white mixture, then fold in the whipped cream.

six Freeze the raspberry mixture in a freezerproof container, uncovered, for 1–2 hours, or until mushy. Turn the mixture into a bowl and stir vigorously to break down any ice crystals. Return to the container and freeze for a further 1–2 hours, or until firm. Cover the container with a lid for storing. Serve in sundae dishes, scattered with raspberries.

Two

three

five

Tarte au citron

Lemon Tart

❖ Serves 6–8
❖ Prepared in 25 minutes,
  plus chilling
❖ Cooks in 35 minutes

Pastry
175 g/6 oz plain flour, plus extra for dusting
½ tsp salt
115 g/4 oz unsalted butter, chilled and diced
1 egg yolk, beaten with 2 tbsp ice-cold water

grated rind of 2–3 large lemons
150 ml/5 fl oz lemon juice
100 g/3½ oz caster sugar
125 ml/4 fl oz double cream or crème fraîche
3 large eggs
3 large egg yolks
icing sugar, for dusting
fresh raspberries, to serve

one To make the pastry, sift the flour and salt into a large bowl. Add the butter and rub it in with your fingertips until the mixture resembles fine breadcrumbs. Add the egg yolk and water and stir to mix to a dough. Gather the dough into a ball, wrap in clingfilm and leave to chill for at least 1 hour.

two Preheat the oven to 200°C/400°F/Gas Mark 6. Roll the dough out on a lightly floured work surface and use to line a 23–25-cm/9–10-inch loose-based tart tin. Prick the base of the pastry all over with a fork and line with baking paper and baking beans.

three Bake blind in the preheated oven for 15 minutes, or until the pastry looks set. Remove the paper and beans. Reduce the oven temperature to 190°C/375°F/Gas Mark 5.

four Beat the lemon rind, lemon juice and caster sugar together until blended. Slowly beat in the cream, then beat in the eggs and yolks, one by one.

five Place the pastry case on a baking sheet and pour in the filling. Transfer to the preheated oven and bake for 20 minutes, or until the filling is set.

six Leave to cool completely on a wire rack. Dust with icing sugar and serve with raspberries.

Mousse au chocolat

Chocolate Mousse

❖ Serves 4–6
❖ Prepared in 10 minutes, plus chilling
❖ Cooks in 6–10 minutes

300 g/10½ oz plain chocolate, broken into small pieces, plus extra finely chopped pieces, to serve
1½ tbsp unsalted butter
1 tbsp brandy
4 eggs, separated

one

Two

one Place the chocolate in a heatproof bowl set over a pan of gently simmering water. Add the butter and melt with the chocolate, stirring, until smooth. Remove from the heat, stir in the brandy and leave to cool slightly. Add the egg yolks and beat until smooth.

Two In a separate bowl, whisk the egg whites until stiff peaks have formed, then fold into the chocolate mixture. Spoon into small serving bowls or pots and level the surfaces. Transfer to the refrigerator and chill for at least 4 hours, or until set.

three Take the mousse out of the refrigerator and serve, scattered with finely chopped chocolate pieces.

Two

Profiteroles

Profiteroles

❖ **Serves 4**
❖ **Prepared in 25–35 minutes**
❖ **Cooks in 40–45 minutes**

Choux pastry
70 g/2½ oz unsalted butter,
   plus extra for greasing
200 ml/7 fl oz water
100 g/3½ oz plain flour
3 eggs, beaten

Cream filling
300 ml/10 fl oz double cream
3 tbsp caster sugar
1 tsp vanilla extract

Chocolate sauce
125 g/4½ oz plain chocolate, broken into small
   pieces
35 g/1¼ oz unsalted butter
6 tbsp water
2 tbsp brandy (optional)

one Preheat the oven to 200°C/400°F/Gas Mark 6. Grease a large baking sheet.

Two To make the pastry, place the butter and water in a saucepan and bring to the boil. Meanwhile, sift the flour into a bowl. Turn off the heat and beat the flour into the butter mixture until smooth. Cool for 5 minutes. Beat in enough of the eggs to give the mixture a soft, dropping consistency.

Three Transfer the mixture to a piping bag fitted with a 1-cm/½-inch plain nozzle. Pipe small balls onto the prepared baking sheet. Bake in the preheated oven for 25 minutes. Remove from the oven. Pierce each ball with a skewer to let the steam escape.

four To make the filling, whip the cream, sugar and vanilla extract together in a small bowl. Cut the pastry balls across the middle, then pipe the filling into the balls.

five To make the sauce, gently melt the chocolate, butter and water together in a small saucepan, stirring constantly, until smooth. Stir in the brandy, if using.

six Pile the profiteroles into individual serving dishes, pour over the sauce and serve immediately.